IMAGES
of America

POTTSVILLE

The small town of Pottsville as seen in a drawing made in 1838. Pottsville grew dramatically during the early decades of the nineteenth century: its population grew from 2,424 in 1830, to 3,117 in 1835, and to 4,345 in 1840. Its trade was no longer driven by the wild speculation in coal lands that had occurred during the 1820s, but had settled into a steady channel, well understood and well managed by capitalists, merchants, and mine operators.

IMAGES
of America

POTTSVILLE

Leo L. Ward and Mark T. Major

ARCADIA

First published 1995
Copyright © Leo L. Ward and Mark T. Major, 1995

ISBN 0-7524-0227-7

Published by Arcadia Publishing,
an imprint of Tempus Publishing, Inc.
2 Cumberland Street, Charleston SC 29401.
Printed in Great Britain

Library of Congress Cataloging-in-Publication Data applied for

Contents

City Hall was located at 14 North Third Street in Pottsville. Borough council held its meetings on the second floor. Notice the gas pump on the sidewalk. Go Forth Alley runs between City Hall and the Pottsville Public Library. The new City Hall was built in 1937, and the building has been the headquarters of The Historical Society of Schuylkill County ever since.

Introduction

Coal was King: so goes the phrase to describe a crucial era in the history of eastern Pennsylvania. During the latter part of the nineteenth century and the beginning of the twentieth, almost everyone who lived between Pottsville, Hazelton, Wilkes-Barre, and Scranton was affected by the daily activity of coal mining.

The first discovery of anthracite coal in what is now Schuylkill County, Pennsylvania, was made by the legendary Necho Allen, a lumberman who lived on Broad Mountain. Allen led a vagrant kind of life, and one night in 1790 he camped out on the wild and desolate mountain, and built a fire among some rocks under the shelter of a small grove of trees.

During the night he felt an unusual degree of heat close to him, and waking up, saw that the rocks were a glowing mass of fire. He had accidentally ignited a vein of anthracite coal. This discovery would lead to the development of the anthracite coal industry in Pennsylvania.

In 1811 Schuylkill County was formed out of Berks and Northampton Counties. By 1818 parts of Columbia and Luzerne Counties were also added to Schuylkill County.

The development of the anthracite coal industry beginning in 1822 caused many fortune seekers to find their way to the county, where the coal mining business was centered in Pottsville. Pottsville became the El Dorado, or the land of riches, for those who came here during the coal rush of the 1820s and 1830s.

The Historical Society of Schuylkill County was founded in 1903 to collect all of the data about the history of the county. Its headquarters are at 14 North Third Street, Pottsville, Pennsylvania. In its photographic collection the society has amassed a wonderful collection of anthracite mining photographs, a few of which are in this book.

Some of the earlier photographs were made by A.M. Allen and his student and protege George M. Bretz. Bretz established his own studio in Pottsville in 1873 and continued to cooperate with Allen. Together they made stereo views of Pottsville and the surrounding area.

Bretz went on to become a world-renowned photographer when he was the first person to take photographs showing the workings of a coal mine using electric lights in 1884, in the depths of the Kohinoor Colliery in Shenandoah, Pennsylvania.

Transportation was the key to opening up the rich veins of Schuylkill County coal to the markets. The Schuylkill Navigation Company's canal reached Pottsville in 1825, and that provided the transportation to take the coal from Schuylkill County to rich markets in Philadelphia. From there coal was transported to New York and New England.

The canal was followed by the Philadelphia and Reading Railroad, which arrived at Mount

Carbon just south of Pottsville in 1842. Within three years the railroad was surpassing the total tonnage shipped on the canal. In the 1880s the trolley system was established in Schuylkill County to link all the towns in the region.

The views in this book are scenes of a bygone era. They are views of anthracite mining and the coal miners who worked in the mines; of canal, railroad, and trolley scenes; and of Pottsville, and its people, places, and businesses.

These views are a small sample of the thousands of photographs that make up the collection of the Historical Society of Schuylkill County. We are sure you will enjoy them, just as we did when we selected the best to share with the people of Pottsville.

Leo L. Ward and Mark T. Major

One
Anthracite Mining

Necho Allen first discovered coal near New Castle in 1790. This c. 1900 image shows the small mining patch of New Castle on Broad Mountain in New Castle Township. The stone house on the left is the Washington House, operated at this time by James Wilson. The road going through the town is the Centre Turnpike. On March 21, 1805, an act of Assembly by the Legislature of the Commonwealth of Pennsylvania was incorporated to build a road that would connect Sunbury with Reading. The Centre Turnpike was constructed over Broad Mountain between 1807 and 1812.

The Girard Colliery was opened on the Girard Estate in 1864 half a mile east of the borough of Girardville. When this image was taken in 1891 it was leased and operated by the Philadelphia and Reading Coal and Iron Company. The tunnel, or drift as it was better known, was dug at the base of a mountain so that the water could run out of the mine. The drift was one of three methods used to mine coal.

The York Farm Colliery was begun in 1836, when a gangway was driven 300 feet into "the bowels of the earth," as the *Miners Journal* poetically expressed it. The slope was one of the three methods of mining that were used in the anthracite coal fields. In 1837, 33,000 tons of coal were sent to market from this slope. The colliery was sold to E.N. Frisbie in 1888, about the time this image was made.

The Pottsville Twin Shafts Colliery represents the third method of mining coal. The shaft went down 1,980 feet where it reached the Mammoth vein. Because of geological faults that prevented successful mining, the shaft was abandoned after being worked for only ten years.

A group of geologists and mining engineers on a field trip to the mines. From left to right are J. Sutton Wall, Baird Halberstadt, John N. Pott, and Anthony W. Sheafer. John N. Pott is the grandson of John Pott, the founder of Pottsville.

A group of breaker boys at the William Penn Colliery near Shenandoah in 1894. It was started in 1864. The company that started it leased about 500 acres on the Orchard, Primrose, Holmes, Mammoth, and Buck Mountain veins. The sinking of the vertical shaft at the colliery was started in 1868 and completed in 1869, and it had a hoisting capacity of about six hundred coal cars a day.

Lining up for a haircut at the outdoor barbershop at the mines near Minersville. The man sitting on the log near the door is obviously next in line. The two men sitting on the bench are playing a game.

From the way they are dressed these men appear to be immigrants from eastern European countries. A large percentage of the increase in population in Pottsville and its environs between 1880 and 1890 was due to immigration from the Slavic countries, such as Poland, Ukrainia, Lithuania, Hungary, Czechoslovakia, and Russia. By 1900, however, immigration into the anthracite coal fields had virtually ceased.

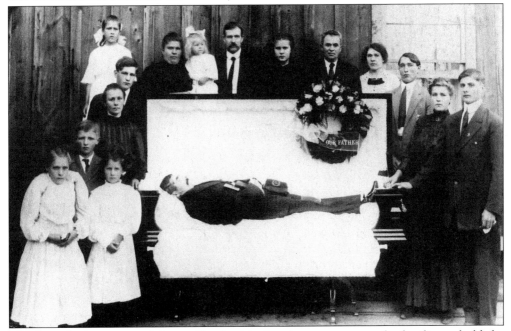

The funeral of a miner in Minersville. At this time it was customary for families to hold the funeral service in the home, and here we can see the mourning family gathered around the head of the household.

Black men gathered at a mine shed. Black people came to the coal region during the 1820s to work in the mines, on the canal, and on the railroads. By 1875 Pottsville, Ashland, North Manheim Township, Tamaqua, Tremont, Barry Township, and Port Clinton all had a very diverse mixture of ethnic groups.

Three miners leaning against a shed at the York Farm Colliery in Pottsville. Notice the carbide light on the hat of the man on the left, and the safety lamps hanging from the belts of the other two miners.

The borough of Gilberton was formed from a part of West Mahanoy Township to the north of Broad Mountain, and was chartered in 1873. It owed its origin to the Gilberton and Draper Collieries as it began as a mining patch. The homes in which the miners lived were built by the operators of the collieries who would then lease them to the miners.

Coal cars are emerging from a mine tunnel in this image. In the early days of mining, horses and mules were used to pull the cars out of the mine, but electric engines came into widespread use as shown here. The miners called these engines "electric mules." They were put into use about 1910.

The Philadelphia and Reading Railroad Company used script to pay its workers. This script was issued in 1879 and 1880 and signed by Franklin B. Gowen, the president of the company. Script was money issued by the company and not by the Federal banking system.

For seventy-one years between 1861 and 1932 the incline railroad plane from Mahanoy Plane to Frackville hauled railroad cars filled with millions of tons of anthracite coal out of the Mahanoy Valley. During its heyday the Mahanoy Plane was one of the greatest tourist sites in the anthracite region, and each year thousands of people came to watch it operating.

16

The Girard Estate offices were located in Girardville as seen in this 1891 image. The Girard Estate owned thousands of acres of coal lands which were originally purchased by Stephen Girard, the Philadelphia financier. It leased the land to operators who would then pay it royalties on the coal that the lands produced.

Once a mule went into a mine to begin its work underground it seldom came out. In this mine a stable was provided for the mules where the hostler or stable boss fed and tended them. Many mules learned to do their work without direction and even to solve problems. When miners died in the mines because of accidents the mules perished with them.

Breaker boys at work at Packer Number 2 near Shenandoah in 1894. The breaker boys picked slate and rocks from the coal as it passed down the chutes. The boys ranged in age from eight to sixteen years old. In 1890 the Mine Inspector reported that 21.6% of the workers at the collieries were boys of this age.

This miner is standing to the rear of a loaded coal car in the Pioneer Tunnel at Ashland. Notice the heavy logs that are used to support the roof of the mine. Today the Pioneer Tunnel is a popular tourist site.

Methane gas was always a deadly hazard for miners. This miner is using his Davy Lamp to test for it. Safety lamps flared up in the presence of methane so they were effective in warning the fire boss and the miner of danger. Although they were not new when miners began to work in Schuylkill County, the problem was always to persuade the miners to use them.

Vaulted arches in an anthracite mine. Starting about 1920 steel and concrete structures replaced timber props in many mines as a safety feature. The miner in the foreground is "spragging" a coal car by putting a log into the wheel. As the wheel turns the log will catch the axle and act as a brake to stop the car.

The blacksmith is putting a new pair of shoes on this mule at the York Farm Colliery in Pottsville, *c.* 1881. Notice the leather leggings that the blacksmith is wearing as he does his work.

"Homeward Bound" is the title of this postcard. Miners' wives used to pick coal on the culm banks near the mines and bring it home to heat their houses during the winter. The kids always went along to help their mothers.

THE DRIVER BOY

Teenage driver boys, such as this one, drove the mules in the mines. Notice the whip hanging around his neck. The driver boys had an unsavory reputation for being coarse-mouthed with their peers and abusive to their mules. As one old operator put it, "The driver is not the sweetest man or boy in the mines. Most of them are profane, harsh, and rough in manner."

A prominent labor leader during the 1902 anthracite coal strike was Mary Harris "Mother" Jones. She led marches for the miners who were striking for higher wages and better working conditions. The strike was called by John Mitchell, president of the United Mine Workers on May 12, 1902. On October 3 President Theodore Roosevelt called both sides to the White House in an attempt to settle the strike, but the meeting was a failure. Following this abortive attempt at reconciliation, Roosevelt threatened to send troops into the coal regions to operate the mines, but also appointed an arbitration commission to try to settle the dispute. The miners returned to work on October 23, 1902, and with the commission's decision on March 22, 1903, the union claimed victory.

This 1925 photograph was taken at the Locust Gap Colliery and shows a head frame with self-dumping cages and a mine car hoist which pulled cars to the top of the breaker where they were automatically dumped. Notice the loaded cars on the way to the top on the middle track while the empties are coming down the left track. The right track was not being used when this photograph was taken.

The employees of the Philadelphia and Reading Coal and Iron Company gathered at the Locust Summit Breaker on October 30, 1946, for this group photograph. This breaker, near Mount Carmel, was the largest in the coal region. It produced coal in various sizes ready for the many markets that were supplied by the anthracite coal industry.

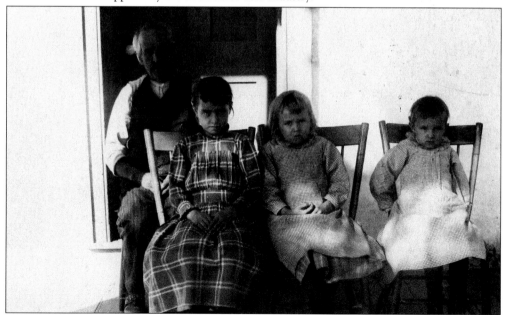

These young girls are daughters of a miner who lived in New Castle, a small mining patch near Saint Clair.

The Saint Clair Colliery was located on the north end of the borough of Saint Clair. It was first known as the Johns Eagle Colliery as it was leased to the Johns brothers, William and Thomas, in 1846. They operated it under the lease until 1872. The colliery was then leased by the Saint Clair Coal Company in 1900 and operated until 1957 when it was closed by the final owner, Gordon Smyth.

The Ellangowen Colliery was located in Mahanoy Township near Shenandoah and was named for the sister of Franklin B. Gowen, the president of the Philadelphia and Reading Railroad Company. By 1881 it had one of the best-constructed breakers in the region and was producing 1,200 tons of coal per day. Two hundred and fifty men and boys worked at the colliery.

The Lincoln Colliery was in the village of Lincoln (near Joliett and Tower City) in the western end of Schuylkill County. This image was made in 1925. That year only about 10,000 tons of coal were produced because of the miners' strike. About a thousand men were employed at the colliery during its peak years.

The Saint Nicholas Breaker was located near Mahanoy City as shown in this c. 1955 image. It was a centralized breaker for the mines in the Mahanoy Valley. Notice the hundreds of coal cars that filled the yard in front of the breaker. This place included the St. Nicholas, Wiggan's, and Suffolk Patches when it was settled in 1861. The post office was established in St. Nicholas in 1863.

Al Gregas of Shenandoah stands with his sledgehammer and a lunch pail waiting to enter a mine as a member of a rescue crew that was battling desperately to save the lives of miners trapped as a result of the Porter-Tower Mine accident in March 1977.

The end of a strike was greeted with cheers by these miners near Mahanoy City as they return to work. Ironically, the miners' frequent strikes ultimately caused consumers to find other fuels, and declining demand brought an end for the jobs of many miners.

A rescue team is carrying the body of a dead miner out of a mine near Saint Clair. Between 1870 and 1993 as many as 30,905 miners lost their lives in mine accidents.

The development of huge dragline machines made it cheaper and more efficient to mine coal from the surface rather than from deep mines, a method known as "strip mining." This image shows the immense size of the buckets that were used to remove the earth above the coal veins.

This photograph, taken at a Reading anthracite stripping operation just south of Heckscherville, shows a dragline shovel in operation in 1978. Huge quantities of earth were moved by these large machines so that the coal could be reached. Fewer men were needed to dig the coal using this method of mining. Draglines were first used in the mid-1940s.

The remains of an abandoned company store in Phoenix Park, a small mining patch near Minersville. These stores were owned and operated by the operators of the mines, who forced all of their employees to do their shopping in them. Of course, the miners would have hardly any pay left after they paid the bills that they owed to their local company store.

This 1940 photograph shows four abandoned miners' homes, the foundations of a fifth, and the remains of Jackson's Patch. A schoolhouse once stood where the rock bank is in the background. The families who lived here stayed until the very end when the road in front was stripped away.

John Siney of Saint Clair formed the first miners' union in the country and led the miners in many strikes to fight for higher wages and better working conditions. Siney became a leader as an organizer in a strike that occurred at the Eagle Colliery in Saint Clair on January 1, 1868. The miners organized a new union called the Workingmens' Benevolent Association of Saint Clair, and the charter was granted by the court in June 1868. In August of that year Siney was elected president of the WBA at a salary of $1,500 per year. The union flourished under Siney's leadership, eventually reaching a membership of forty thousand in Schuylkill County. Siney's struggles for the miners ended with his death in Saint Clair on April 16, 1880.

John Siney's counterpart on the side of capital was the colorful and flamboyant Franklin B. Gowen. Gowen was the district attorney of Schuylkill County during the Civil War, attorney for the Philadelphia and Reading Railroad Company, and ultimately president of the railroad company. Under his leadership the company began buying coal lands in 1871, and by 1880 it owned 160,566 acres, thus controlling the production of coal and its transportation to market. Gowen was responsible for bringifng the Pinkerton Detective Agency into the county to infiltrate and destroy the "Molly Maguires," a secret society of Irish miners who murdered mine superintendents. He also appeared as a prosecuting attorney in the sensational "Molly Trials" of 1876. Twenty "Mollies" were convicted and hung for "Molly Maguire" murders and crimes. Gowen mysteriously committed suicide in a Washington hotel room in 1888.

John L. Lewis, president of the United Mine Workers, is shown here speaking to a group of college students visiting Pottsville in 1951.

As mines went deeper ventilation became a problem for the men who worked underground. Technology was used to develop and install these huge fans that brought fresh air into the mines and drew out the stale air.

This steam-powered diamond drill was manufactured by the Pennsylvania Diamond Drill Company of Pottsville. The company was organized on October 20, 1869, in Reading but it was soon moved to Pottsville. The diamond drills that it manufactured were used to drill through the heavy rock over coal veins.

The Girard Colliery was located on the southern edge of the borough of Girardville. The land that the colliery was developed on was part of the Girard Estate which leased it to Cornelius Garretson on May 1, 1863. The breaker in this image was erected during 1863–64. In 1866 the lease was transferred to Theodore Garretson who was operating it when this image—a classic photograph by George M. Bretz—was made in 1874.

Four miners holding their mule during a strike at the Wadesville Shaft Colliery in 1926. The Wadesville Shaft Colliery was under construction in 1884, but building had to be suspended in 1885. It was kept on standby status for fifteen years and was then reopened in 1900. It continued to operate until the 1930s.

This 1888 photograph shows some miners' homes in Duncott, a small mining patch near Minersville. The miners who lived in these homes worked at the Oak Hill and Pine Hill Collieries. Author Leo L. Ward's father was born here in 1900, and his grandfather, Christ Ward, lived in Duncott and was a fire boss for twenty years at the Oak Hill Colliery.

This image shows the "stripping" of the huge Mammoth vein near Shenandoah. Notice the gangways that were dug into a vein when it was deep mined. This stripping is on the site of the Shenandoah City Colliery where work was begun in 1862. The buildings on the site—including forty-seven tenant houses and a large boarding house—were completed in 1863.

The wives of some local miners are dressed in their finest in this *c.* 1900 photograph made in Girardville, and their efforts at sophistication certainly brighten up their surroundings. Apparently they were having an afternoon tea party. The woman in the middle wearing a black dress is a very striking person.

A rotary railroad car dump at the Saint Nicholas Breaker, *c.* 1955. A railroad car would be put into the cylinder and turned upside down to dump the coal. This method of dumping coal at the breaker made the operation extremely cost efficient.

The Bear Ridge Colliery was located near Mahanoy Plane in the Mahanoy Valley. This breaker was built there in 1871 by George F. Wiggan and C.H.R. Treiblesn and had a capacity of 450 tons daily. This is another of George M. Bretz's classic images—Bretz was noted for having people pose in his images.

This image, taken at the Morea Colliery near Frackville, is considered a classic coal region scene. Note the negative number on the right. This indicates that it is probably a Bretz image, since he carefully put negative numbers on the glass plates that he made.

These miners are gathered at the Wadesville Colliery for a group photograph. The Wadesville Shaft was started in September 1864 and completed on May 31, 1867. In 1872, Horace Greeley, the prominent New York editor and politician, came to Schuylkill County and visited the colliery, but disaster struck just five years later, on May 9, 1877, when a major explosion of firedamp in one section of the mine killed six men and injured six others. Unfortunately, such accidents were an all too common feature of life in the mines, and were both abhorred and accepted as part of the industry.

These remains of the abandoned Saint Clair Coal Company represent the end of an era in Schuylkill County coal mining history. In the early days of mining in Saint Clair it was known as the Johns Eagle Colliery, and it was worked until 1957, when owner Gordon Smyth decided to cease operations. When it was torn down it became the site of a huge stripping operation.

Two
The Schuylkill Canal

The northern terminus of the Schuylkill Canal was Port Carbon after the canal was extended from Mount Carbon to Port Carbon in 1828. As this section of the canal was busy, this sketch—drawn looking west toward Pottsville—was probably very fanciful.

So much coal dirt washed into the canal at Dam No. 1 at Port Carbon that it was the first to be abandoned—wharves, landings, and all—in 1853. Ruined wharves along the Pottsville-Port Carbon road are pictured here, c. 1860.

This rare old image of the Schuylkill Canal at Connor's Crossing near Cressona was made when the canal waters were placid and deserted. The railroad bridge that is being built in the background was for the Pennsylvania Railroad that was pushing its way north to Pottsville, where it arrived in 1886.

An abandoned canal lock at Connor's Crossing near Cressona. Notice the tunnel of the Pennsylvania Railroad bridge on the right. Today Route 61 from Schuylkill Haven to Pottsville crosses this site, and the Cressona Mall is nearby.

Canal boats lined up above and below the Broadway Bridge in Schuylkill Haven. The bridge connected Dock Street with the Irish Flats. H.S. Paul, a Philadelphia photographer, took this view looking north from Saint Peter's Street, c. 1878.

Dam No. 7 and Guard Lock No. 13 were at the beginning of the canal in Schuylkill Haven, effectively at the upper end of Saint John Street. A frame house, which served as the canal's clearance office, stood here prior to 1860.

The Dundas dock was built in 1846. The Lippincott dock, named for Joshua Lippincott, a past Schuylkill Navigation Company president and manager, was completed in 1853. It had a water frontage of 3,368 feet. Each landing within a dock was equipped with a coal pocket, chutes, scale, office, tracks, and switches. The docks were served by the Mine Hill Railroad and the Schuylkill Haven Railroad.

PORT OF POTTSVILLE. CLEARANCES.			
July Aug	Boats	Despatched by	Tons
5	Catawissa	T Mills	28
	Delaware	Dill	33
5	Black Bird	T Mills	36
	Penn Township	N Nathans	20
	J C Wynckoop	Shippen & co	34
	Red Rover	Heser	22
7	Thomas Haht	Russell	29
	Ridgway	Morris	25
	Lydia	Russell	32
9	Elizabeth	Do	26
9	L B Clark	Do	30
	Fanny	Ortlip	17
	Swan of Ches co	Kline	16
10	Hoogly	Dennis	30
10	Columbia	Do	24
	Swan	Shippen & co	23
	W C Barber	Russell	34
	Centreville	Do	32
	J B Patterson	P & Patterson	34
	A Reed	Russell	30
	De Witt Clinton	Baily	28
	R E Griffith	Russell	26
	S B Reves	Do	30
	Vincent Pilot	Kolb	26
11	Phineas	Russell	25
	Geo Laudell	Do	28
	Thos Hoskins	Dill	33
	Jane	Morris	26
28			770
PORT CARBON.			
Aug			
5	J Q Adams	Brook & co	30
6	Fancy	Wetherill	32
	Mary	Turbert	28
6	North Branch	Bashyshell	23
	Mill Creek 1	Smith	30
	Mill Creek 2	Do	29
7	Java	Brooke & co	23
9	Shamrock	Smith	30
10	C Benjamin	Wetherill	29
10	W Lawton	Bli Wid & co	33
	Margaetta	Smith	29
	Hellen	Wetherill	28
	Sarah Ann	Do	28
	Lady Washington	Brooke	28
	J Hacker	Do	32

The *Miners Journal* published weekly lists of canal boats leaving from the ports of Pottsville and Port Carbon. The listings gave the date of departure, the names of the boats, their owners, and the weight of coal they were carrying. Benjamin Bannan kept statistics on the coal trade for more than forty years.

Great Luck.

B. Bannan has sold the following prizes in the Union Canal Lottery within the last six weeks.

10, 52, 57, ¼ a prize of $6,000
16, 31, 40, ¼ in 12th class 1,000
8, 16, ¼ in 50

Besides numerous prizes of $40, 30, 20, 10,

THE UNION CANAL LOTTERY,
CLASS No. FOURTEEN
Draws on Saturday next, July 14th 1822.

SCHEME.

1	Prize of	$30,000
2	do	10,000
4	do	5,000
10	do	1,000
1	Prize of	640
20	do	600
46	do	300
51	do	200
51	do	100
51	do	50
102	do	40
102	do	30
1,479	do	20
11,475	do	10

TICKETS $10—Shares in proportion—for sale at the office of the

MINERS' JOURNAL.

Lotteries are nothing new, as is seen in this advertisement for the Union Canal Lottery. This advertisement is taken from an 1829 edition of Benjamin Bannan's *Miners Journal* newspaper. Bannan once entered a lottery (and won, luckily enough) to keep his newspaper from going out of business.

This image of the canal in Schuylkill Haven was made by G.D. Green of Pottsville, sometime between 1881 and 1886. The view is looking south from Lock No. 12, Dam No. 7. To the right is the Lippincott dock. A large number of boats are tied up along the towpath above and below the Broadway Bridge.

This canal boat is stranded in front of Motzer Bakery and Mengel's Butchershop in Schuylkill Haven, c. 1880. Notice the boy standing in the bed of the canal at the front of the boat. The company boat is located almost in front of what was then the mule yard. Today the Parkway begins at this spot.

John Bausman, locktender at Lock No. 12, weighed over 400 pounds. He died in the shed adjacent to the lock, a shed that was built especially for him since he could not fit through the lock house door. When he died the shanty had to be torn down to get his body out.

Warner's boatyard was in what is now the Edgewood Addition of Schuylkill Haven, as seen in this c. 1885 image. A large boat is under construction in the center of the photograph, while a number of boats awaiting repairs are moored nearby. To the left (to the right and rear of the new boat) is a boat lying in dry-dock.

The first tunnel in North America was dug through this hill near Landingville by the Schuylkill Navigation Company. Built between 1818 and 1819, it was 450 feet long, 20 feet wide, and 18 feet from the canal bottom. The canal horses and mules would walk over the hill while the boats poled through the tunnel. By 1837 the tunnel was cut to half its length, a decade later it was widened and again shortened, and finally, between 1855 and 1860, the roof was removed.

The canal boat *Bruce* coming up the Blue Mountain Dam at Port Clinton on August 15, 1906. The Schuylkill Canal was built as slack-water navigation—trenches dug for the canal constituted about 50 miles of its length, while the other 50-mile stretch was made up of dams that were used to back up the water.

The Schuylkill Electric Railway, running between Schuylkill Haven and Palo Alto/Mount Carbon, was built on the towpath of the Second Mountain part of the canal. This image was taken facing east on April 2, 1910, and shows the remains of Lock No. 8.

This image, taken on August 18, 1905, shows a combination coal washery and stern wheeler that was used in getting coal from the riverbed in Felix's Dam No. 19 between Leesport and Reading.

This dredging machine in the Hamburg level was used to make repairs to the towpath, which had been broken through in a number of places by the cloudburst of August 3, 1906. This image was made on August 15, 1906.

The canal boat *Bird* approaching the Blue Mountain locks near Port Clinton. This image was made on August 2, 1912 by H.C. Wilson of Schuylkill Haven. Wilson was an amateur photographer who made many images of canal scenes in the early 1900s.

The Little Schuylkill Railroad, serving the coal fields around Tamaqua, terminated at the Port Clinton loading docks. Coal was then shipped to various markets on both the canal and the Reading Railroad. In 1916, 17,000 tons of coal, carried by a fleet of approximately 30 boats, was shipped on the canal, a dramatic drop in cargo from the peak of 208,000 tons handled in the 1850s.

A wreck boat is quietly plying its way along the canal, c. 1880. Smoke is coming from its boiler stack, showing that it is propelled by a steam engine fueled by anthracite coal. Notice the mirror image of the boat in the water.

The canal boat *Bruce* was built in 1879 in Landingville, and had a 103.77 gross tonnage. Philadelphia was its home port. The *Bruce* is shown here in the Big Blue Mountain Dam pool on its August 15, 1906, journey to Port Clinton. Notice that the captain of the boat is "hitching" a ride on one of the mules trudging along the towpath.

The *Petrel* was one of many canal boats that carried almost everything, including passengers. A typical fare was $2.50 for the trip from Reading and Philadelphia (or Philadelphia to Reading), and this fare included meals, but not a berth.

This *c.* 1880 image of South Centre Street, Pottsville, looks out over the Schuylkill River as it wends its way around the "Island" where the Atkins Iron Works was located. The Schuylkill Canal and the bridge that crosses from Mauch Chunk Street to Palo Alto can be seen in the upper center section of the picture. The Pottsville Hospital is in the upper left of the picture and a barren Greenwood Hill appears to the left.

This stereoscopic view was taken by Pottsville photographer A.M. Allen and shows Benjamin Haywood's Palo Alto Iron Works from Dam No. 2, Lock No. 2. The canal boats in the foreground are anchored at Young's Landing. The landing is on the east side of Pottsville where Anderson Street meets Route 209 as it enters Pottsville, from Port Carbon.

Employees of the Schuylkill Navigation Company standing in front of the Navigation Building on Coal Street, Schuylkill Haven, c. 1886.

OVERLOOKING SOUTHEASTERN POTTSVILLE FROM SHARP MOUNTAIN (ABOUT 1890)

We can ascertain that this photograph, looking from South Centre Street toward Mauch Chunk Street in Pottsville, was taken before the Pennsylvania Railroad arrived in Pottsville in 1886 as only the earlier Reading Railroad tracks can be seen. Greenwood Hill is in the upper center of the picture, with only one home on it.

This image was made on July 1, 1945, and it shows what was left of Lock No. 30 (located 1/4 mile north of Hamburg) after the canal had been left to deteriorate. William H. Dietrich is the man standing on the bridge. The lock was 100 feet long, 14 feet wide, and about 20 feet deep. The picture was taken by Gerald Sherman, a civil and mining engineer based at 4 West 43rd Street, New York, New York.

This was all that was left of the canal boats 1/3 mile north of Hamburg on July 1, 1945. A man from the neighborhood is standing on top of the boats and William H. Dietrich is standing on the canal bed. For many years people from Schuylkill County who drove on the road between Port Clinton and Hamburg could see the remains of canal boats, but today they are all gone.

Three
Railroads

The Reading Company Passenger-Freight station on Union Street in Pottsville. Originally located at Mount Carbon, the station was moved to Union and Railroad Streets a short time after the line moved into Pottsville. The station at Union Street was opened in 1851.

The artist who made this painting describes it as, "From Pottsville on the banks of the Schuylkill which is here seen through the Gap of Sharp Mountain commences the canal and railroad landing. Mount Carbon is on your left at the foot of which is the Great Hotel of that name." The canal reached Mount Carbon in 1825, and was the key to unlocking transportation from the Schuylkill coal fields to the tidewater markets at Philadelphia.

As business moved uptown it was necessary for the railroad station to be nearer the center of things so the Reading Company built this Queen Anne-style station on East Norwegian Street. On June 21, 1887, the new station was formally opened for use. The honor of running the first train out of the station fell to the Good Intent Fire Company who chartered a special train to run them to Atlantic City.

The Pennsylvania Railroad station on East Norwegian Street was formally opened on November 18, 1886. The railroad then continued to push its way to the collieries in the northern part of the county, reaching Shenandoah by December 19, 1887.

A group of excursionists at the Mount Carbon station in May 1880. The men are officials of railroads who were touring anthracite mines in Schuylkill County.

Reading Railroad yards in Pottsville on a snowy winter day—February 27, 1961.

A train runs into the Reading Railroad station in Pottsville on April 10, 1949.

Schuylkill County's link with Dauphin County was the Schuylkill and Susquehanna Railroad. In this photograph one of the railroad's early locomotives, the "Lark," has stopped for a photo opportunity at East Norwegian and Railroad Streets, Pottsville, in 1866. The Norwegian House on the right opened around 1844, and, under the ownership of James Gough and his wife Hannah, continued until 1867. The other sign is that of a blacksmith shop, while in the background are the premises of Pomroy & Son, iron manufacturers. Greenwood Hill forms part of the skyline.

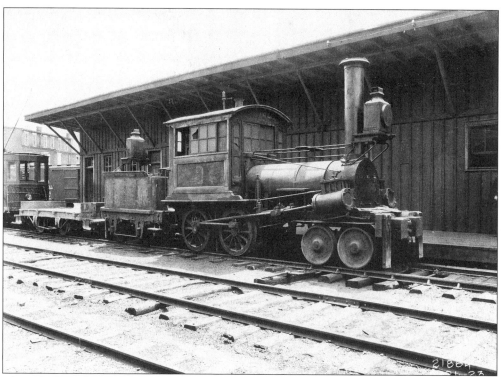

The Lehigh Valley Railroad at the 12th Street station in an image made on May 24, 1923.

Workmen were putting the finishing touches to the Pennsylvania Railroad bridge at Mauch Chunk Street when this historic picture was taken, looking east on Mauch Chunk Street, on March 20, 1886. Even in the days before the automobile, busy streets could be a problem in a growing town—here two drivers of a two-horse team wagon and a horse and buggy are causing somewhat of a traffic jam in the same block of the dirt street..

The Pennsylvania Railroad bridge being built over Dock Street in Schuylkill Haven, *c.* 1886.

A Pennsylvania Railroad track crew laying the final stretch of track on Coal Street as the railroad reached its passenger terminal in Pottsville in 1886. Today Route 61 has replaced the Pennsylvania Railroad at the site.

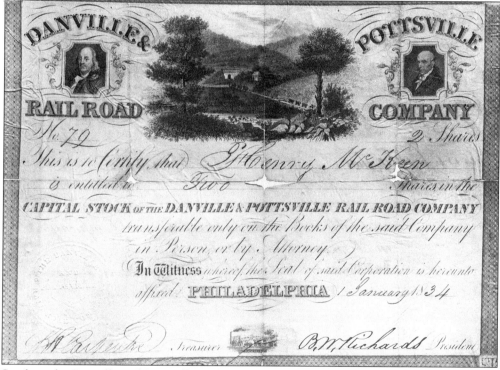

Stock in the Danville and Pottsville Railroad dated January 1834. In 1830 Stephen Girard, a Philadelphia financier, purchased 17,362 acres of prime coal land in Schuylkill County. Girard purchased the land at public auction on April 17, 1830, because he was convinced that it had valuable coal reserves. He was one of the backers of the Danville and Pottsville Railroad, but he died in 1834 and the line was never completed.

Trains coming into Pottsville on the south side of town. The Reading Railroad tracks make a "Y" as they come into Pottsville and the right-hand tracks continue to towns north of Pottsville. The Pennsylvania Railroad entered Pottsville on the tracks to the right that come over the bridge and then cross the "Island" at Atkins Iron Works.

A Pennsylvania Railroad engine crossing the trestle at the "Island" as it comes in front of Atkins Iron Works.

A Pennsylvania Railroad engine in front of the Philadelphia and Reading Coal and Iron Company shops on Coal Street in Pottsville. Notice that the engineer is wearing a straw hat—it must have been a hot summer day.

Engine No. 770 is shown with its crew on board in this George Bretz image. The date and the members of the crew are unknown, but it is still an outstanding Bretz photograph.

The first train to cross the Lehigh Valley Railroad trestle at Connor's Crossing in 1890. The trestle was torn down and today the Cressona Mall is on the site to the left of the Schuylkill River.

The Landingville coal storage yards of the Reading Railroad are shown in this rare image.

Probably one of the rarest images in the collection of The Historical Society of Schuylkill County is this photograph of the Pennsylvania Railroad yards at Mount Carbon. The men with silk toppers were typical of railroad officials of the day. In the left center is the old covered bridge which connected the Philadelphia and Reading Railroad with the Pennsylvania Railroad.

The Pennsylvania Railroad yards at Mount Carbon. The bridge crossing the Schuylkill River connected the Reading Railroad with the Pennsylvania Railroad. It burned down in 1935.

Loaded coal cars at the Pennsylvania Railroad yards at Mount Carbon. Each car contained about 80 tons of coal.

The Pennsylvania Railroad tunnel at East Mines near Saint Clair. After the railroad reached Pottsville in 1886 it continued its drive to reach the towns and collieries in the northern part of Schuylkill County, and this tunnel was dug to run the line up Broad Mountain.

Railroad hoboes making a stew near Palo Alto on October 25, 1885. It was probably a delicious meal for the two men.

Building a Pennsylvania Railroad bridge at Darkwater on November 3, 1887, as the railroad advanced up Broad Mountain to Frackville.

The ladies coming from the train at the Reading Railroad depot in Frackville do not look like they had a particularly good trip in this image.

GEO M BRETZ, Photographer, Pottsville, Pa.

Negatives Nos. 27409—27410.

Philadelphia & Reading R. R. and Coal & Iron Police Quarters,
Gordon, Pa., Feb'y 23rd, 1888.

1 LIEUT. JOHN HARRIS,	6—GEO. CAMPBELL.	11—FRANK GRAEFF.	16 WM W FAUST
2 C T LYON,	7—MAHLON ALLENBACH.	12 SEB DANIEL.	17—CHAS W CRAMER
3 H C MILLER.	8 WM SHRAGEN,	13—CHARLES BECKLEY.	18 M P STUTZMAN
4 LEE BERRY,	9 W S GROFF.	14 JOHN J SIMMET.	19 WM SCHNEIDER

A George Bretz image of the Philadelphia and Reading Coal and Iron Company Police at Gordon on February 23, 1888. Gordon was an important railroad town, and there must have been trouble there in 1888. Notice that the cook is also carrying a gun.

The Shoemakersville train wreck occurred in 1890 and involved a freight train and a passenger train. With a death toll of twenty-two, it was the worst wreck ever on the Philadelphia and Reading Railroad.

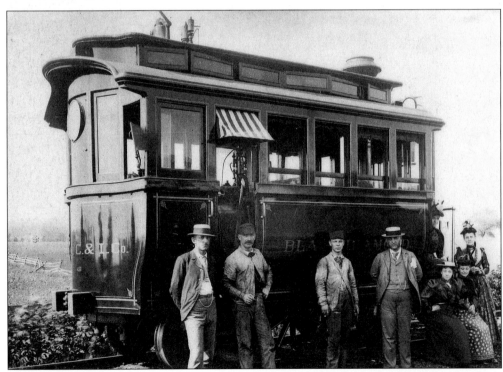

The Philadelphia and Reading Coal and Iron Company's "Black Diamond" was a special car used by railroad officials.

An all-Lehighton crew manned diesel No. 580 as the Lehigh Valley Railroad wound up the Pottsville Division on April 3, 1953. Posing with their engine at the 12th Street are, from left to right: (bottom row) Joseph F. Snell (flagman), Harry W. Dotter (conductor), and Wilbur J. Getz (trainman); (top row) Elmer Rupell (fireman) and Adam Haydet (engineer).

Steam locomotive "1956," one of the first to go out of service at the Reading Railroad's Saint Clair yards, stands silent at the coal dock as workmen prepare it for shipment to the Reading yards for dismantling. The "Iron Horses" were retired as new diesel engines took over the Saint Clair yards.

The Saint Clair yard of the Reading Railroad was opened in 1913. The yard was the largest classified rail yard in the country. In its heyday it had a capacity of 2,101 cars and a total track length of 46.26 miles. The yard employed 1,020 men, and the car shops were equipped to make all repairs. The roundhouse was large enough to contain fifty-two locomotives.

A Pennsylvania Railroad train rounds the corner near the Pottsville gas house at Centre and Nichols Streets as it returns from a trip to Fishbach. It probably picked up a shipment of freight at the Aetna Steel plant on Peacock Street in Pottsville.

The Locust Summit Breaker near Mount Carmel was built by the Philadelphia and Reading Coal and Iron Company in 1930. Coal trains are assembled in the yard in the upper right of this image. The breaker was closed down in 1954.

Engine No. 47 was the first buckwheat coal burner to use Wooten's patent. It is shown here at the Frackville Scale Office.

THE PHILADELPHIA, READING, an POTTSVILLE RAIL ROAD.

WAS opened for Passenger Travel, and the general Transportation of Merchandize on *Thursday, January 13th, 1842.*

WINTER ARRANGEMENT.

Hours of Starting of Passenger Trains.

From Pottsville, at 8½ A. M.
From Philadelphia, at 9 A. M. } Daily.

Hours of Passing Reading.

For Philadelphia, at 10½ A. M.
For Pottsville, at 12½ P. M. } Daily.

Both Trains passing at Pottstown.

FARES,

Between Pottsville & Philada.	1st Class.	2d Class.
" Orwigsburg "	3,50	2,50
" Port Clinton, "	3,25	2,30
" Hamburg "	3.00	2,25
" Reading "	2,75	2,00
" Douglassville "	2,25	1,75
" Pottstown "	1,75	1,25
" Phoenixville "	1,50	1,10
" Norristown "	1,00	0,75
" Reading & Pottsville,	0,50	0,40
	1.40	1,00

The Philadelphia and Reading Railroad arrived in Pottsville in 1842. This is the timetable for passenger service for that year. Within three years the railroad had overtaken the canal in terms of coal tons shipped to market.

The Schuylkill Canal was frozen when the "Catawissa" arrived from England in 1833, so it was taken apart and hauled by ox-cart to Tamaqua. The "Catawissa" and the "Comet" were the first engines in the nation to transport coal regularly and they operated between Tamaqua and Port Clinton on the Little Schuylkill Railroad.

Lehigh Valley Railroad engine No. 74 stops at Park Place near Mahanoy City so a photograph can be taken of the trustees of the Girard Estate. The estate owned coal lands in northern Schuylkill County and leased them to coal operators who paid the estate royalties on the coal that was produced. The trustees would make annual visits to inspect the holdings of the estate, such as this trip in 1891.

The Soldiers and Sailors monument designed by artist and sculptor August Zeller was dedicated on "Monument Day," October 1, 1891, to honor the thirteen thousand men from Schuylkill County who served in the Civil War. The Pennsylvania Railroad brought eight thousand visitors to Pottsville that day and one of its trains is seen unloading its passengers in this image. The Reading Railroad brought eight thousand people, and the Lehigh Valley Railroad brought five thousand more for the great day.

Welcoming the circus train as it unloads in the Pottsville yards of the Reading Railroad, *c.* 1900. The circus parade would start here and end at the circus grounds, and crowds of people would watch the parade pass through town. The elephants were always a highlight of the parade.

The head of the Mahanoy Plane is seen in this image. Huge engines pulled coal cars up the plane from 1862 until it was finally closed down in 1933.

These mining officials are posing for a photograph in a Philadelphia and Reading Railroad car at the foot of Big Mine Run Plane near Ashland, *c.* 1891.

The end of the line!

Four
Trolleys

A key event in Schuylkill County trolley car history came on November 2, 1892, when the Eastern Pennsylvania Railway Company organized and took over the franchise of the Tamaqua & Lansford Street Railway Co. By 1906, it had taken control of all trolley service in the county. The trolley cars were housed in the Pottsville Union Traction Co. car barn (shown here) in Palo Alto.

Car No. 44 sits on the rails outside the Palo Alto car barn. The big fire of January 6, 1917, destroyed the power plant and the car barn of what was then the Eastern Pennsylvania Railway Company. The whole region was in darkness for ten hours as a result of the fire.

Car No. 36 is cut in half at the car barn to make it larger.

Here Car No. 36 has "grown" in the middle to make it bigger.

Not all the trolley cars in the county were built at the Palo Alto car barn. Car No. 22 of the Ashland & Centralia line was built by the J.G. Brill Company of Philadelphia.

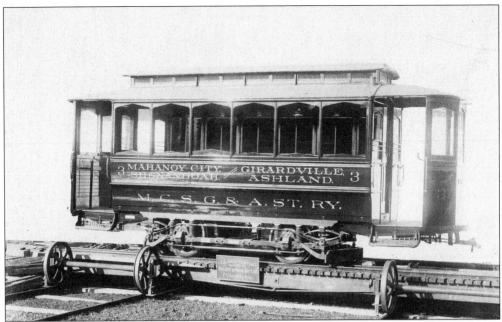

This trolley car was built by the J.G. Brill Company for the Mahanoy City, Shenandoah, Girardville, and Ashland line.

Laying double track on South Centre Street in Pottsville. The gang boss, in his white shirt and vest, is closely directing the brick-paving crew while someone from the front office, in full suit, is scratching his head in wonderment over some unidentified action. Even though the two homes that sit on the terrace to the left are not visible, the steps and walks that lead up to them are still a familiar sight on South Centre Street.

Another view of the tracks being laid on South Centre Street; this time looking toward the Sheafer Building (now the YWCA). Here we can see the two houses on the terrace and the 1895 Evangelical United Methodist Church on the right. Sylvester Produce is on the left.

A crew laying track at the corner of North Centre and West Market Streets. The Thompson Building is on the left, and the L.C. Thompson Hardware Store is on the northwest corner of West Market Street. The Schuylkill Trust Building was built on the site of the Thompson store in 1924.

A double track being laid on North Centre Street between Arch Street and Race Street. The Exchange Hotel is at the southwest corner of North Centre and Arch Streets. Today the site is a parking lot for the Meridian Bank.

Car No. 316 has been commandeered as a loco for those three dump cars. The condition of the rails and ties suggests paving has been removed on North Centre Street near Minersville Street to prepare for double tracking. The Family Restaurant on the right is offering a "Special Dinner 25 cents."

The tracks are all laid and the crew has gone to work in another town. This trolley car is traveling up North Centre Street toward the 1863 Female Grammar School.

The tracks have been laid on South Centre Street and a two-car trolley is off to Tumbling Run with a crowd of pleasure seekers.

The trolley rounds the "Y" at Palo Alto as it turns to go to Tumbling Run. The car on the left is coming from Port Carbon and will soon be on South Centre Street in Pottsville.

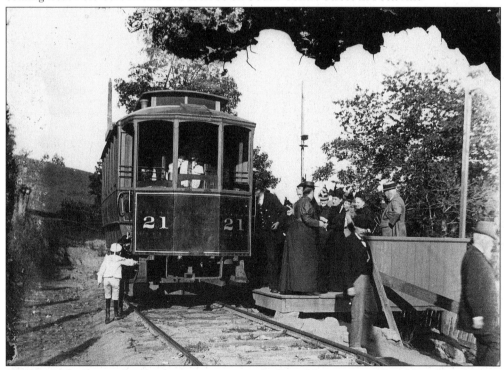

Car No. 21 loading and unloading passengers at the Boat House stop at Tumbling Run. Notice the little fellow on the left waiting to get on board. The conductor on the right is helping the ladies off the trolley.

At last, the end of the line is reached at the Tumbling Run Hotel. Tumbling Run was the talk of Pennsylvania for a period of thirty years. Schuylkill County's playground was to be found in the Tumbling Run Valley, where two immense storage dams that were built to supply the Schuylkill Canal supplied the setting for one of the most beautiful and attractive summer resorts in the state.

The Yorkville trolley brining passengers back to Pottsville from Tumbling Run on September 11, 1894. The old Tumbling Run Hotel can just be made out on the right. The sign on the old open-air car is advertising "Baseball Today" at the Tumbling Run ballpark.

Here is car No. 36 (the same car we saw being made larger at the Palo Alto car barn on pp. 88–89) in service on its way to Yorkville. There was a "Big Show" at Tumbling Run that week. William Berger (left) is the conductor and William Werner is the motorman.

The Gilberton Trolley Riot occurred on July 21, 1893, when the Gilberton Borough Council and the Schuylkill Traction Company had a dispute concerning the location of track within the borough. The borough tore up 200 yards of track, and the Schuylkill Traction Company brought in a "dinkey" that had picks, shovels, and rifles for a show of force. Councilmen Reynolds and Stone met with the "dinkey" crew and told them that the tracks could be only relaid with picks and shovels, not rifles. Then, satisfied that trouble had been averted, they dropped into Foley's saloon. Shots rang out, however, and in the melee two men were killed.

The "Trojan" removing snow from the trolley tracks at Adamsdale after a big snow storm.

Two trolleymen and seven passengers pause to pose for a photographer as the old "High Baller" of the Schuylkill Electric Railway Company stops at the intersection of Union Street and Saint John Street in Schuylkill Haven. Trips in these open air cars were a popular pastime at the turn of the century.

The Schuylkill Haven trolley pauses for a minute to have this image made while the passengers on board look out the window at the lens of the camera. "Darkest America" is playing at the Academy of Music and admission is only 50¢ as advertised on the sign in the front of the trolley.

Three trolleys are rounding a curve near New Philadelphia on August 17, 1906, as a man stands in the road watching for the cars to arrive.

Three trolleys stop in Garfield Square near the Soldiers and Sailors monument for this unique image. The monument was dedicated October 1, 1891. Notice that no work had been started around the base of the monument where a park had been planned. That dates this image as being about October or November of 1891.

NOTICE TO PASSENGERS

On and after this date all Large Dogs and Hunting Dogs will be carried on front platform of cars or in the baggage department of combination cars. Conductors will collect full fare for each dog, the same as a passenger. Small dogs carried on passenger's lap same as a child will be carried free of charge.

RESPECTFULLY,

Schuylkill Electric Railway Co.,

A "Notice to Passengers" by D.J. Duncan, Superintendent of the Schuylkill Electric Railway Company, dated October 13, 1898.

A trolley car passes through Garfield Square on June 30, 1932, the last day of trolley service in Pottsville. The last car left Minersville at midnight and was run to the Palo Alto barn by Motorman George Heiser and Conductor George Hutchinson. Bus service started in town the next day.

The Capitol Bus Company provided service between Pottsville and Harrisburg as seen in this four door bus that has stopped by the Soldier and Sailors monument in Garfield Square.

The Pottsville Bus Terminal is at the site of the old Pennsylvania Railroad station on East Norwegian Street. It opened for passenger service in 1950. The old Pennsylvania Railroad YMCA is seen on the left.

Five
Pottsville Scenes

This "View of Part of the Borough & Environs of Pottsville, Schuylkill County" was sketched by T.P. Ashwin, a Philadelphia architect who had come to Pottsville in the summer of 1830 to supervise the erection of a number of fine residences. The view that he drew is looking west from Sharp Mountain over South Centre Street and Pioneer Island toward Port Carbon. The Schuylkill River is winding its way along Mauch Chunk Street on the left, and the Schuylkill Canal is running along the base of Sharp Mountain on the right.

George M. Bretz came to Pottsville from Carlisle, Pennsylvania, as a student of A.M. Allen about 1870. In 1873 he set up his own studio at the southeast corner of North Centre and East Market Streets. Even though they were competitors, Bretz and Allen collaborated to make stereos and views of Pottsville and the collieries of Schuylkill County. Bretz was famous for making photographic images in a coal mine by using electricity. The studio shown in this photograph burned down in a disastrous fire in 1892 resulting in the loss of thirty thousand of Bretz's negatives.

In 1852 A.M. Allen came to Pottsville from Deerfield, Massachusetts, and established himself in the photographic business. His studio was at the southwest corner of West Market and North Centre Streets as shown in this c. 1881 image. The Historical Society of Schuylkill County has a collection of the early photographs and stereoscopic views that he made from the 1850s onwards.

The Mortimer House was built in 1823 by Peter and Jacob Seitzinger as a private dwelling. Colonel George Shoemaker bought the building about 1824 and opened a hotel there, continuing the business until he sold the property to William Mortimer, Jr. It was then sold to the Mountain City Banking Company in 1875, and torn down soon after. The Pennsylvania National Bank is now located at the site on the southwest corner of West Norwegian and Centre Streets.

The North Western Hotel was at the northwest corner of North Centre and Laurel Streets, and its proprietor was C. Sheetz. This image was made on a fine summer day in the 1890s—there was no business being done inside because all of the customers were outside posing for the photographer. The Park Hotel was built on this site in 1897.

This 1880s photograph of a quiet morning on Centre Street was taken at 10:16 a.m (as can be seen on the clock in front of Mortimer's store). A wagon loaded with produce is disappearing off the left of the picture while the man in the street crosses behind it. It looks like business is slow for R.J. Mills, Hatter.

The *Evening Chronicle* was located at the northwest corner of Railroad and East Norwegian Streets. The Chronicle Publishing Co. was organized in the spring of 1875 and on April 17 of that year the first ever edition of the *Evening Chronicle* was published, with Solomon Foster, Jr., as editor. The paper cost 1¢ and its purpose was to establish an evening paper for the town of Pottsville and to furnish the Democratic party with a daily organ for reaching the people. The *Chronicle* continued publication until September 1923.

Work on the Washington Street bridge was started under the direction of Chairman Baird Snyder, a city councilman. The abutments for the bridge were completed on November 30, 1888, and the bridge was opened for traffic on February 21, 1889, and then formally opened on March 1, 1889. The bridge was closed to traffic in 1987.

Councilman Joseph Hummel was the first to drive over the Washington Street bridge, followed closely by George M. Smith. The Pennsylvania Railroad and the Philadelphia and Reading Railroad each contributed $10,000 to its construction. Its total cost was $18,932.08. Notice the stairs leading down to Coal Street, now Route 61.

A huge International Order of Odd Fellows arch was erected for a celebration in the borough of Pottsville. This photograph was taken looking south on Centre Street from West Market Street. There were no automobiles on Centre Street that day, only horses and buggies.

Even before Henry Clay's towering monument had been dragged up South Second Street to its pillar overlooking southeastern Pottsville, Joseph Silver conceived the idea that the site was ideal for the town's first office building. And so he built a row of offices along the side of the hill and connected it with a large terrace, dubbing it the Silver Terrace. Today the Sheaffer Building is on the site on South Centre Street.

Proud and stately, the *Miners Journal* building looms over South Centre Street on the site of the old Silver Terrace. It was a reproduction of Town Hall, Bradford, England, and was built for $125,000 by Colonel Robert M. Ramsey, publisher of the newspaper. Work on the structure was begun in August, 1874. On October 29, 1892, it burned to the ground, and became just a memory to the borough's awed citizens.

The statue of Henry Clay, here seen from the porch of John Bannan's Cloud Home, looks down over Pottsville in this image. When the statesman died on June 29, 1852, the citizens of Pottsville erected the monument in his memory because he advocated a protective tariff in his famous American System that would protect American industries from imports from Great Britain. A tariff was placed on many imported products from Great Britain, including iron, that protected the iron industry, giving impetus to the interests of Schuylkill County iron founders and to the anthracite coal industry.

August Zeller came to Pottsville in 1887 to carve a monument to the 96th Pennsylvania Volunteer Infantry that stands on the battlefield at Gettysburg. While here he designed and sculpted the Soldiers and Sailors monument which was dedicated in Garfield Square on October 1, 1891. Here he is at work on the Genius of Liberty, which stands on top of the monument, in his studio in Koppitsch's Hall on Mauch Chunk Street. Today the studio is the site of the parking lot for the Pottsville Hospital.

And here is Zeller's great work standing in Garfield Square on a placid day in Pottsville. Note that there is not a trolley, an automobile, or a person in the scene. The photographer must have made this image early in the morning. Also note the wreath of flowers at the base of the Spanish-American War monument.

110

The milestone on the old Centre Turnpike was put there many years ago. It reads "35 to R," or 35 miles to Reading. It was first put on the east side of South Centre Street, but was then moved to the west side near the Henry Clay monument.

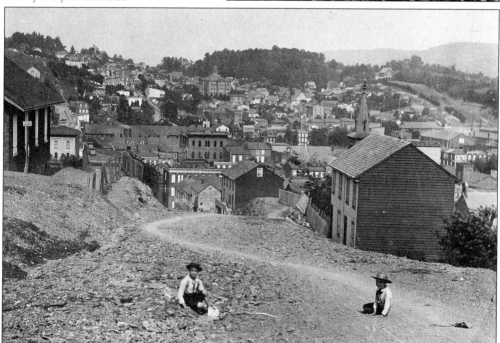

Two little boys are playing in the dirt of High Street (now Race Street), which was not only one of the hilliest parts of Pottsville, but was high above at least some of its houses. At the left is the old Race Street School building which was destroyed by fire about 1900. In the middle of the image can be seen Centennial Hall, which was destroyed by fire, and the Jackson Street School stands in the upper middle of the image.

North Centre and Nichols Streets looking down from North Second Street. Nichols Street was named for Pottsville's first chief burgess, Francis Nichols. David Neuser's stockyard was located at the corner of Coal and Nichols Street. The tracks of the Pennsylvania Railroad run under the bridge, so this dates the picture in the late 1880s. The Stockyard Hotel was established in 1872, and was located near Coal and Nichols Street. The Good Will Fire Company was built on Nichols Street in 1898.

"Mom, I want a ride on the Ferris wheel," was the cry from the kids in Garfield Square during the 1906 Pottsville Homecoming Days. Flags and strings of electric lights are stretched across the square for the festivities. "Tickets 10 cents for the Grand Stand," reads the sign on the right. The stand was erected for the great homecoming parade that was held that week.

The Mountain City building was built in 1875 on the site of the old Mortimer House at the southwest corner of Centre and West Norwegian Streets. The *Miners Journal* had its headquarters in the building after its ornate building burned down on South Centre Street in 1892. Moses Phillips started making shirts on the fourth floor of the building in 1898. His little shirt company grew into the famous Van Heusen Shirt Company.

Ground for the new First United Methodist Church was broken on this site at Fourth and West Market Streets in August 1902. Miss Ann Hill, the oldest member of the church, was allowed to drive the first pick. The cornerstone was laid on November 1, 1903. The great day for the Methodists, the dedication of the magnificent new church, came on September 17, 1905.

The L.C. Thompson hardware store is being torn down at the northwest corner of West Market and North Centre Streets to make way for the new Schuylkill Trust Building that was built in 1924. The business was established by Stichter & Thompson in 1855. "Out we Must go by April 1st," reads the sign. Some familiar Pottsville businesses can be seen in the advertisements painted on the buildings. Hummel's Furniture store and Malarkey's Music Store are among them.

One of the earliest hotels in the history of Pottsville was the White Horse Tavern or Hotel, which was located on this site at the southwest corner of Centre and Mahantongo Streets. The little tavern was constructed about 1818 by George Dengler. The hotel went through many hands, and became known as the Merchants Hotel. On February 14, 1898, Thomas G. Allan purchased it, replaced the frame structure with a brick building, and changed the name to the Allan Hotel, as seen in this June 1926 image before it was torn down to make way for the new Necho Allen Hotel.

The Necho Allen Hotel has been topped out beside the *Daily Republican* building in this 1927 image of the new community hotel. Notice the two men sitting and standing on the girders near the top of the structure. The site at the southwest corner of South Centre and Mahantongo Streets has long been the location of hotels in Pottsville, including the White Horse Tavern or Hotel and the Allan Hotel.

The Necho Allen Hotel was completed and dedicated as seen in this November 1, 1927 image. It was a landmark building and was noted for its famed "Coal Mine Tap Room." The hotel was a community center in Pottsville, serving the social needs of the town for many years. It was closed in 1982, and today it is used as apartments for senior citizens.

The history of the site of the Pennsylvania Hall Hotel dates back to 1817 at the point where five log cabins were erected by Henry Donnell at the northwest corner of South Centre Street and Howard Avenue. The hotel was built in 1830. It was opened to the public on July 11, 1831, by Colonel George Shoemaker, and served that function for 127 years until it was torn down in 1958. Its spacious dining room was the scene of many fine banquets, as well as civic and patriotic events.

Schuylkill County was created on March 18, 1811, when an act allowing for its creation from part of Berks and Northampton Counties was approved. The act provided that courts be held in the tavern of Abraham Reiffsnyder in the tiny hamlet of McKeansburg until a court house was built in Orwigsburg in 1815.

One of the area's old landmarks, the Phillips taproom at the Mount Carbon Arch, was purchased by the Pottsville Building Block Company in April 1954 to make way for a storage area. Known as the Knickerbocker Hotel, it dated back to 1836. Mr. and Mrs. Phillips are standing on the porch as they prepare to bid good-bye to the old structure.

This diner sat at the northwest corner of Minersville and North Centre Streets until it was torn down in 1937 to make way for the new City Hall. The Diner Garage is right behind it going up Minersville Street toward the Court House. The Sailor Planing Mill and Lumber Company office and yard was near the Pottsville Hospital in those days. The truck parked on the street has a sign on it that reads "Fine Foods." It was 2:40 p.m. on the Court House clock when the photographer made this image.

The new City Hall was built in 1937 at the northwest corner of Laurel Boulevard and North Centre Street. The colorful Claude A. Lord was the mayor of Pottsville at that time. The clock that stands in front of it is no longer there. It once stood in front of a jewelry store on Centre Street between West Norwegian and West Market Streets.

It was 1948 and Governor Thomas Dewey of New York was running against President Harry S. Truman when this election banner flew over Centre Street. Ivor D. Fenton of Mahanoy was running for a seat in the United States House and Paul L. Wagner of Tamaqua was running for a spot as a state senator. They both won in the election, but Dewey did not, as President Truman beat him in a big upset.

The Court House in Orwigsburg was of brick and was two-stories high. The court room was on the first floor, and the jury rooms and public offices were on the second floor. The first court was held in it in the spring of 1816. The cost of the building was $5,000. After the courts were moved to Pottsville an academy called the Arcadian Institute was established in the building in 1854. It soon failed and the building was leased to the Orwigsburg Shoe Manufacturing Company in 1873.

A lot was purchased between Second and Third Streets in the northern part of Pottsville from the estate of George Farquhar, and work on the new Court House was started in October 1849. The total cost of the building was $30,000. The judges of the court in May 1851 certified to the commissioners the satisfactory condition of the Court House, and in December 1851 it was officially opened for business. The Schuylkill County jail, which stands on Sanderson Street to the left of the Court House, was erected in 1853.

By 1891 a new and larger Court House was erected, and here we see the old and the new standing beside each other. The site of the old Court House is now used as a parking lot. The impressive architecture of the building looms over Pottsville, and its clock tower tells the time of day for the citizens of the town. In the 1930s Orphans Court was added to the west side of the building. That part of the Court House is now used as the offices of the Board of Commissioners, and other offices.

Six
People and Places

The Mansion House in Mount Carbon opened on May 19, 1832, and was torn down—after almost a century of service—in the 1930s. It was a favorite summer hotel for the wealthy of Philadelphia who came for the mountains and the salubrious air of Schuylkill County. Many banquets were held in the hotel to celebrate the great events that were happening in the coal industry. Notice the horse-drawn trolley on the right.

Pottsville was one of the stations of the Underground Railroad that smuggled escaping slaves north to Canada. James Gillingham, a Friend in the Society of Quakers, lived in a brick house at the northeast corner of Seventh and Mahantongo Streets. He hid the slaves in his basement by day and helped them to escape by night.

The George L. Schreader Pottsville Granite and Marble Works was located at 537 North Centre Street, Pottsville. Schreader was a skilled craftsman who carved the Grecian urn that supports the Genius of Liberty atop the Soldiers and Sailors monument in Garfield Square. His middle name was Lincoln because he was born the day that President Abraham Lincoln was assassinated.

Miss Edith Patterson came to Pottsville in May 1918. She served as the librarian of the Pottsville Free Public Library for thirty-two years and gave her invaluable assistance to everyone from schoolchildren, students, and researchers to authors, poets, and historians. She became an authority on the history of Schuylkill County, especially the Molly Maguires.

The Third Brigade Band is a Pottsville institution that was officially formed in 1881, although it actually dates back to 1849. This photograph was taken c. 1909. The band has headquarters on the second floor of the Historical Society of Schuylkill County's building, but the band itself spends most of its time playing (and marching) in concerts and parades.

The Pottsville Post Office stood for many years at the southwest corner of West Norwegian and South Second Streets. This 1936 image was made just before it was torn down to make way for the new post office that would be constructed on the same site. The building on the left is the Philadelphia and Reading Coal and Iron Company. The eagle on the top of the flagpole on the roof of the post office is now in the Historical Society of Schuylkill County museum.

And this is the post office that replaced the old one. It was dedicated in 1937 by Postmaster General James Farley, who served under President Franklin D. Roosevelt. A huge crowd attended the dedication ceremonies. The "new" post office is now used as an office building.

The great Pottsville fire of 1914 destroyed a large two-story brick building that housed the Academy of Music and Union Hall. When the Academy of Music opened on January 17, 1876, it was rated one of the finest playhouses of its size in Pennsylvania. An additional attraction for the audience was Grady's Saloon, located in the basement. The thirsty playgoers would slip into Grady's between acts, and would be summoned back by a tinkling bell when the curtain was raised for the next act.

Ted Bushar and his famed Sauer Kraut Band, shown here with leader Ted and his ax baton, marched in the Philadelphia Mummer's Parade from 1907 to 1921. The band was always in the limelight in the Quaker City extravaganza and brought home many prizes. Two of their favorite songs were "Turkey in the Straw" and "Ach du Lieber Augustine."

It is a quiet day at the Tumbling Run Hotel in this vintage image. The motorman and conductor of the trolley are waiting to begin their run back to Pottsville with the summer fun-lovers. The two buggies are waiting for their sleepy passengers to come out of the hotel for a brisk drive in the pines.

Boathouses—some owned by clubs and some by individuals—ran along the north bank of the second dam of the Tumbling Run resort. Some folks moved from town to their boathouses for the warm weather while others kept them just for entertaining.

These boys are "skinny dipping" into the Tumbling Run lake from the roof of the steamboat that took people on rides around the lake for 5¢. Boys will be boys. We wonder if the boys paid for the ride? Maybe it was free the day this image was made in 1896.

The Long Run Hotel was a favorite stopping place for travelers between Schuylkill Haven and Pine Grove. Riding parties would stop at the hotel for sumptuous country meals, and sleighing parties liked to take advantage of its warm fireplace during the winter.

The staff of the *Pottsville Journal* newspaper poses for the photographer in front of its 213-215 South Centre Street headquarters on the paper's 100th anniversary in 1925. Seated in front are H.G. Rhoads (general manager) and H.L. Silliman (owner). The young man on the left peeking between the two girls is cub reporter John O'Hara, who left the paper to become a famous novelist.

Pottsville celebrated its Sesqui-Centennial anniversary in 1956, and this is the board of directors posing in the Henry Clay Room of the Necho Allen Hotel. A lot of the men grew beards and mustaches for the celebration. Howard S. Fernsler, business manager of the Pottsville School District, is the man in the front row wearing a white coat, and Mayor Michael Close is seated on the far right in the front row.

Two young ladies are dressed in the height of fashion as they stroll along East Norwegian Street just east of Coal Street in the 1890s. The Philadelphia and Reading Coal and Iron Company Shops are seen in the background. Notice the brick sidewalk, the trees, and the dirt road.

As a wonderful comparison, here are two Pottsville young ladies dressed in the height of fashion at the same place—but this time in the 1940s. The sidewalk is now concrete, as is East Norwegian Street. There are cars parked on the street, and the Pottsville Shops are still there. The girl on the left is Lola Evans who graduated from Pottsville High School in 1945.

The Capitol Theater opened its doors on Monday evening, November 21, 1927. A crowd of over three thousand gathered that opening night to see the brilliant new theater, and the audience gasped in admiration at the beauty of the richly-appointed theater. *My Best Girl*, starring Mary Pickford, was the feature picture. The Capitol Theater is gone, and the site is now occupied by a parking deck.

A policeman is directing traffic in front of the Pennsylvania National Bank in May 1966. The Hollywood Theater has been turned into a drive-in for the bank that sits on the site that has at various times been home to the old Mortimer House and the Mountain City building. The Necho Allen Hotel is in the background.

The YMCA was built in 1911 at the northwest corner of Second and West Market Streets. All the boys in Pottsville and the surrounding towns came to the "Y" for the athletic activities that were conducted there. As with many other spots in Pottsville, the site that used to be home to the "Y" is now a parking lot. This image was made during World War II.

These boys and girls are in a "Fun Run" that had its starting line in front of the Female Grammar School on North Centre Street. Ah, the exuberance of youth!

William F. Cody, better known to the world as "Buffalo Bill," is the gentleman in the carriage wearing a cowboy hat as he guides his two-horse carriage through Garfield Square on his way to the circus grounds. This image was made about 1910. The man in the carriage with him is Bench Miller of Pottsville, who saved Buffalo Bill's life from Indians on the Western Plains. Buffalo Bill's circus came to Pottsville every year.

By an act of assembly of the Commonwealth of Pennsylvania approved on April 4, 1831, Schuylkill County was made a poor district. Being a poor district meant that the county could legally put paupers (poor people) into the Alms House. Alms Houses in Pennsylvania were known as "poor houses." On April 9, 1831, the county purchased 226 acres of land on the Centre Turnpike in North Manheim Township, about 1 mile south of Schuylkill Haven, for $6,000. When the farm was first purchased the tavern house standing alongside the turnpike was used as the almshouse until the main building was erected in 1833. Penn State's Schuylkill campus is on the site today.

Seven

Businesses

D.G. Yuengling was born in Wurtemberg, Germany, in March 1806. He was educated there, and at the age of twenty-one came to the United States. He settled in Pottsville in 1829, and immediately commenced brewing about five barrels of strong beer a day in his Eagle Brewery. Today the Yuengling Brewery is still identified with the qualities of strength and pride, symbolic of the American Eagle.

The kegs look the same, but the mode of transportation for beer is different these days than back when this photograph was taken in front of the Yuengling Brewery on Mahantongo Street. The first brewery burned down shortly after it was started, and Yuengling then located his brewery here, where there was an ample supply of good water. Caves were dug into Sharp Mountain behind the brewery to keep the beer cold. The brewery is the oldest in the United States, and has been managed by five generations of the Yuengling family. Today Dick Yuengling is the president.

A prize of $5,000 was to be awarded to the first foundry to successfully use anthracite coal to smelt iron for three months. In 1839 the Pioneer Furnace on the southern edge of Pottsville was the first foundry to do so. The breakthrough encouraged iron foundries to use anthracite coal, and caused much demand for coal throughout the Schuylkill Valley.

Before the coming of the supermarkets every neighborhood in Pottsville had its own grocery stores and meat markets, as well as more specialized stores and services. This photograph shows one of these stores, Schmall's Meat Market, on September 21, 1890. Paul Umbenhauer is the small boy holding a ball in the middle of the picture. He died from diphtheria a month after this picture was made.

This driver was in no hurry to pull from the curb with his turn-of-the-century furniture from the Gately and Britton Store at 210 West Market Street. The Dalmatian under the wagon turned only slightly when the photographer's camera clicked. This image is, all in all, a fine study of leisurely activity in front of the store of Ed Gately and George Britton in the "hitching post era."

The tally-ho is waiting in front of the D.L. Esterly Store in this 1863 image. It looks like some of the young boys are hoping to get a ride in it. Notice the hoop skirt that the woman in the middle is wearing. The store was built at the northeast corner of Centre and Mahantongo Streets in 1830. Today it is the site of the Schuylkill Chamber of Commerce.

Jacob Ulmer, like D.G. Yuengling, was born in Wurtemberg, Germany. He learned the butcher's trade in Germany before coming to the United States, arriving in Pottsville on July 2, 1854. He opened a very successful butcher shop on North Centre Street and in 1873 built this packing house at the corner of Front and Railroad Streets in the Jalappa section of Pottsville.

The Miners National Bank, established in 1828, was the first bank in Pottsville. This photograph shows the original bank building before a new building was erected in 1927. The bank's business has increased over the years, and, in a recent merger with another bank, it changed its name to the Heritage National Bank.

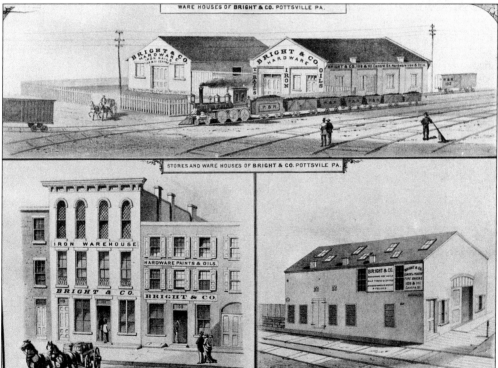

The coal mines of Schuylkill County did a great deal of business with the local hardware stores, and one of the largest of them was Bright & Co. of Pottsville. The store was located at 109-111 North Centre Street in Pottsville, but it also had warehouses, one of which was located at the corner of East Norwegian and Railroad Streets.

Jesse Fleet's variety store was built in 1894 at 10 South Centre Street in Pottsville. Notice the rocking horse on the sidewalk. All the kids who walked by the store must have gone for a ride on it. It looks like Jesse was having a sidewalk sale the day this image was made, because there is merchandise on the tables in front of the store. The store burned down in 1906.

The lower shops of the Pottsville Casting & Machine Shops were located at the southeast corner of East Norwegian and Coal Streets. The Pottsville Shops were formed in 1882 by the Philadelphia and Reading Coal and Iron Company to make machinery for the thirty-seven collieries they owned. The shops were closed early in the 1950s and then torn down.

John Raring's shoe store stood on south Centre Street beside Clemens Drug Store. The family lived above the store. The store supplied footwear to customers throughout the county. Many country people would only buy their shoes from John Raring, and would travel to Pottsville whenever they needed shoes.

Employees posing in front of Hummels furniture store on North Centre Street (near the Pottsville armory). Hummels' slogan was "You marry the girl, we'll furnish the house."

The Pottsville Board of Trade was organized during the late 1880s to encourage a silk mill to locate in Pottsville and bring new jobs to the town. On May 31, 1887, it was announced that the Tilt Silk Mill would come to Pottsville. The building was erected in 1888. At the peak of the mill's success, 1,500 employees spun silk cloth on 2,000 looms.

Employees posing for the camera at Krieg & Bros., 309 North Second Street, c. 1900. Krieg & Bros. supplied lumber and hardware to its many customers in Schuylkill County. Irvin Krieg, the owner, is the man with the mustache sitting in the carriage.

It is opening day at the new Dives, Pomeroy, and Stewart Department Store at 100-104 South Centre Street in Pottsville, and the employees are posing for a commemorative photograph. Pomeroy's, as it came to be known, was a county institution at this location for many years. When the malls came to Schuylkill County it moved to the Schuylkill Mall near Frackville.

Always an essential service for heavy industry and particularly for coal mining, blacksmith shops were among the earliest businesses in Pottsville. This building on North Centre Street (beside the Schreader Marble & Granite Works) was one of the last surviving blacksmith shops in town. Centre Street was a dirt road when this image was made. The houses in the background are on North Second Street.

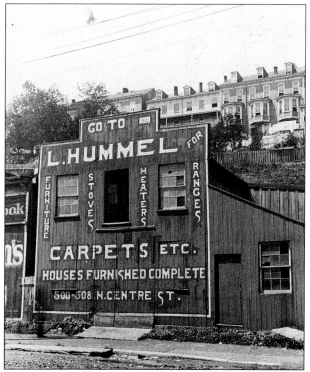

In 1874 F.P. Mortimer opened his dry goods store at 1 North Centre Street. Ladies could sit at the counter in Mortimer's store to pick the cloth that they wanted to use to make their dresses or other clothing. From five to ten ladies were employed on woolen knit goods, which in the winter season had a large demand. Notice that all the women employees are wearing high-collar blouses.

A general view of Pottsville looking west from Lawton's Hill. Coal Street can be seen in the foreground and just behind Coal Street are the Buechley Lumber Yards. The Court House is looming over the town from its location on North Second Street.